fabric art
workshop
Susan Stein

fabric art
workshop
Susan Stein

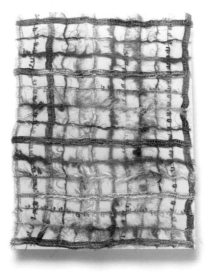

Exploring techniques and materials
for fabric artists and quilters

**Creative Publishing
international**

Minneapolis, Minnesota

acknowledgments

Thanks to so many wonderful friends—Diane Bartels, Laura Murray, Mary Johnson, Wendy Richardson, Shelly Stokes, Elizabeth Palmer-Spilker, and Sue Kelly—who have opened my eyes to the joys of playing with fabric in new ways; to students who have taught me a lot more than I have taught them; to my husband, John, who encourages me always; and to Linda, Joanne, and Sharon at Creative Publishing international, who have always believed in me.

Artwork Attributions

Page 2
Autumn Glow; Sampler Quilt
Susan Stein
Minnesota Historical Society, Permanent Collection

Page 6
Journal Class Sampler
Susan Stein

Creative Publishing
international

Copyright © 2007
Creative Publishing international, Inc.
400 First Avenue North
Suite 300
Minneapolis, MN 55401
1-800-328-3895
www.creativepub.com

Printed in China
10 9 8 7 6 5 4 3 2

Library of Congress Cataloging-in-Publication Data

Stein, Susan.
  Fabric art workshop : exploring the latest techniques and materials /
Susan Stein.
    p. cm.
Includes index.
  ISBN-13: 978-1-58923-328-7 (soft cover)
  ISBN-10: 1-58923-328-X (soft cover)
  1. Altered books. 2. Fabric pictures. 3. Textile fabrics. I. Title.

  TT896.3.S78 2007
  702.8'1--dc22
  2007007251

President/CEO: Ken Fund
Vice President/Sales & Marketing: Peter Ackroyd
Publisher: Winnie Prentiss
Executive Managing Editor: Barbara Harold
Acquisition Editors: Linda Neubauer, Deborah Cannarella

Development Editor: Sharon Boerbon Hanson
Production Managers: Laura Hokkanen, Linda Halls
Creative Director: Michele Lanci-Altomare
Senior Design Manager: Brad Springer
Design Managers: Jon Simpson, Mary Rohl
Director of Photography: Tim Himsel
Lead Photographer: Steve Galvin
Photo Coordinators: Joanne Wawra, Julie Caruso
Book Design: Tina R. Johnson
Cover Design: Jon Simpson
Page Layout: Tina R. Johnson
Photographer: Andrea Rugg

FABRIC ART WORKSHOP
by Susan Stein

Permission to reproduce the printed images from Carol Belanger Grafton, ed., *Authentic Chinese Cut-Paper Designs*, Dover Design Library (New York: Dover Publications, Inc., 1988), used in Printout to Fabric Transfer, granted by Dover Publications, Inc.

Due to differing conditions, materials, and skill levels, the publisher and various manufacturers disclaim any liability for unsatisfactory results or injury due to improper use of tools, materials, or information in this publication.

table of contents

i can do that with this?

With busy lives and lots of distractions, taking a little time out to **play**, to **create**, to find out **"what if"** – is important.

These small and portable projects make catching some creative time easy. Designed as "journal pages," they are fun to do at group get-togethers and with kids. They also require very little equipment.

The idea for making fabric journal pages began during a Quilt Market in Houston. Among all the gorgeous quilts, wall hangings, and garments were small pieces that chronicled people's lives throughout a year. Some included writing and poetry, but typically the page alone conveyed a message. It was an arresting exhibit because it was so unusual and personal. Inspired, I began to teach a journal class to explore innovative techniques for, with, and on fabric. I encouraged students to pick a theme that held meaning for them, both to express themselves and to contribute unity to their collection of pages. You'll see a haiku journal, a dragonfly-dusted wall hanging, and autumn-as-inspiration pieces in the Artists' Gallery at the back of the book.

Who knew we would paint fusible web, make beads from fabric, and take worms out of cocoons? But new ideas pop up constantly and the only thing stopping fiber artists from trying something is the desire to do it all right now!

Fabric Art Workshop takes you through 27 techniques that use paint, fiber, embellishments, and even copy machines to make personal pages. These can then be used for wall hangings, fabric books, matted pieces, screens large and small, boxes, and anything else your imagination can devise. You may find yourself inspired to create larger pieces that combine several of the techniques, or perhaps you'll apply the artful approaches to enhance garments.

In preparation for making the projects, collect the best paints and fabrics you can find. Prepared-for-dyeing (PFD) fabric is ideal for any painting technique; it has no sizing or finish to interfere with good paint absorption. You will find PFD fabrics at fine quilt shops. For all of the projects, you will want to start with pieces of fabric cut at least 9" x 11½" (22.9 x 29.2 cm) so you have a little "insurance" while working or for seam allowances. After you complete a piece, you can trim it to the finished book size, 8½" x 11" (21.6 x 27.9 cm), unless you plan to mat it or sew it onto another piece of fabric.

I used paints by Jacquard for many of the methods in *Fabric Art Workshop*. They layer well and offer a range of possibilities: Dye-na-Flow,® a thin transparent paint, behaves almost like a dye; Textile Colors,® a medium-bodied paint, also gives transparent coverage; Neopaque® colors are opaque; and Lumiere® colors are metallic. Embellishments I found everywhere—even at the hardware store!

The makers of some of the products used with certain techniques never intended (or imagined) such uses, so be prepared for unexpected results! Many techniques should be tried a couple of times before using them to make a final project piece. Write notes with a permanent marker on the edges of practice pieces to record what you did. Turn a mistake into a happy accident whenever you can.

Keep a file of test samples (and articles and resources) so you can easily find them when you want them. Be mindful of safety precautions when using products like bleach or when melting synthetic materials; work outside when possible or work in a vented room. Most of all, cultivate a playful attitude and be ready for the question *"How* did you DO that?

Susan L. Stein

angelina fiber

Angelina is different from any other fiber you've seen.

It melts together into a luminous flat sheet that can be used as created, cut into shapes, trapped behind netting, sewn as an appliqué, adhered to fabric with paint, fused to fabric, or embossed with stamps.

Create bowls and other vessels using it as a stand-alone material, or combine it with other fibers for felting or silk fusion. A highly reflective, polyester fiber, Angelina adds sparkle to water or sky even in minute amounts. For extra pizzazz, add threads, sequins, or bits of silk into the fiber before fusing. Experiment and have fun! This fiber opens many possibilities for you.

After creating a sheet of Angelina, try burning the edges or burning through it with a heat tool or candle flame. Pressing Angelina with an iron changes its color—a process you manage by controlling the heat. The more heat, time, and pressure you use when you iron the Angelina, the more the color changes. Be sure to always use a piece of cooking parchment over and under the fiber whenever applying heat.

materials and tools

Hot-fix fiber: Angelina

Cooking parchment
(available at grocery stores)

Iron

Stamp: rubber, acrylic, wood, or foam, with bold, deep design

Sheer fusible web: Misty-white Fuse

Fabric

angelina fiber

Angelina fiber offers four techniques **to use alone or layer** into one intriguing page.

Preparation

Before you begin, read through all of the techniques described in this section. One technique may contain a detailed instruction that is necessary for related techniques.

Fuse the Fibers

Place a thin layer of fibers on a piece of parchment. Cover them with another sheet of parchment. Set the iron to the temperature for silk and briefly press over the top of the parchment. Check the fibers to see if they are fused together and press a little longer if they are not. If the color changes more than you like, turn down the temperature of the iron and try again. Trim the edges of the fused piece if you desire.

Create a Stamp-Embossed Shape

Place a stamp right side up on the ironing surface. Arrange the fibers on top of the stamp. Put a piece of parchment on top of the fibers and iron for a few seconds. Check the fibers to see if the image of the stamp is embossed into the surface. To change the color of the image while leaving the surrounding fibers the original color, leave the iron on the stamp a little longer. Trimming the uncooked fibers off the edges is optional.

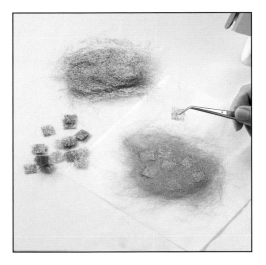

Make Shapes

Place a thin layer of fibers on a piece of parchment. Cover them with another sheet of parchment. Briefly melt the fibers into a sheet that barely holds together. Cut it into squares, triangles, or any shape you like. Place a layer of uncooked fibers in a contrasting color on a piece of parchment, arrange the shapes on top and cover with another very thin layer of the fibers. Cover with parchment and iron to fuse everything together.

Form a Fusible Appliqué

Layer a piece of parchment, a 9" x 11½" (22.9 x 29.2 cm) piece of fusible web, fibers, and another piece of parchment, in that order. Iron to fuse the layers together, but stop before the colors change. Cut the fused-fiber sheet into strips. Weave the strips together on top of the piece of fabric. Cover the fibers with parchment. Carefully turn the fabric over and iron quickly from the back to fuse the fibers to the fabric.

Susan Suggests

Angelina is washable and fun to use on a garment. Additional heat applied to the fibers will continue to change their appearance, so hand-wash your garment and dry it flat.

A good resource for additional information is *Between the Sheets with Angelina* by Alysn Midgelow-Marsden.

paintstiks technique quartet

Artists have used paintstiks—linseed oil and pigment solidified into a stick form—for many years.

Versatile, easy to use, and permanent when set properly, they come in many colors and a wonderful array of iridescent hues. A blender stick—a colorless stick used for making value gradations—allows you to create lighter colors. You can purchase paintstiks individually or in sets.

Now that the fiber people have discovered them, paintstiks have become a very popular tool for decorating clothing, wall hangings, cloth books, and art dolls.

Apply the color directly to the fabric—it's just like coloring with a crayon. You can use paintstiks to make rubbings of fairly flat objects that have recesses deep enough to feel through fabric, or try one of the many commercial rubbing plates. Stencil using a stencil brush and any purchased stencil design (or make your own stencil from freezer paper or template plastic). Use masking-tape guides to paint straight lines for plaids. Pull the color off of a paper with torn edges to create lovely, soft stripes.

Clean hands and brushes with citrus cleaner, workshop solvent, or soap and water. Protect your carpet and your clothing, as any flakes of paint that fall from your work surface will dry and become a permanent stain.

materials and tools

Plastic cover for the table

Nonslip surface: Grip-n-Grip

Masking tape

Fabric: washed and ironed to remove sizing and wrinkles

Paintstiks: Shiva Artist's Paintstik

Paper towels

Small knife

Rubbing plates

Stencils

Bristle stencil brushes: ¼" (6 mm) or ½" (1.3 cm)

Iron

Cooking parchment (available at grocery stores)

Kraft paper

Cardstock

Double-stick tape

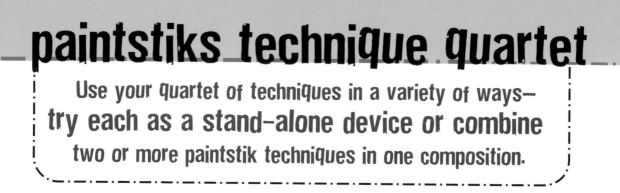

paintstiks technique quartet

Use your quartet of techniques in a variety of ways—
try each as a stand-alone device or combine
two or more paintstik techniques in one composition.

Preparation

Protect your work surface with the plastic cover. Before you begin, read through all of the techniques described in this section. One technique may contain a detailed instruction that is necessary for related techniques.

Write or Draw

Place the nonslip surface on your table. Using masking tape, adhere three edges of the fabric to the surface, right side up. Peel off the protective skin that forms on the outside of the paintstik, either by pinching it off with a paper towel or trimming it off with a small knife. When the stick glides easily over a piece of paper, it is ready to use. Write words or draw abstract lines on the fabric with the paintstik.

Note: If the paintstik wears down to the cardboard cover, loosen the cover around the stick and push the stick up from the opposite end, leaving the cardboard intact.

Make a Rubbing

Slide a rubbing plate under the fabric through the open edge. Stroke over the fabric with the flat end of the paintstik to capture the pattern from the rubbing plate. Move the plate as needed and continue to stroke the paint onto the fabric. You can use more than one color if you like, but be careful not to smudge already painted areas. You will, with a little practice, be able to avoid stroking off the edges of the rubbing plate.

Stencil

Tape a stencil to the fabric or hold it firmly in place. Choose a brush size appropriate to the stencil openings. To smoothly load your stencil brush with paint, first stick a large piece of masking tape to your work surface, then rub the paintstik onto the back of the tape. Load the brush by picking up as much paint as possible from the tape. Brush the color from the stencil edge into the opening to create a soft outline that lightens toward the motif center.

Note: You can create a stencil from freezer paper! Cut out a shape, leaving approximately 2" (5.1 cm) of paper as a surround. Iron the paper, shiny side down, directly onto the right side of the fabric.

Create Soft Forms

Tear strips of cardstock. Apply double-stick tape to the back of the strips, and place them on the fabric where you want to create a stripe. Stroke a paintstik onto the paper and then brush the paint from the torn paper edge onto the fabric to make a soft stripe. Repeat for as many stripes as desired. To mix colors, apply your paintstiks to a large piece of masking tape or rough paper and then mix the paints with your brush.

Finishing

Let the fabric dry for at least two to three days. If you try to work with it earlier, the paint will smear. Set an iron to the correct temperature for the type of fabric you are using. Protect your ironing surface with a piece of parchment or kraft paper. Iron the back of each area for 10 to 15 seconds.

Susan Suggests

To give an appliqué a three-dimensional effect, draw around it with a paintstik to create a shadow.

foiling four ways

A bit of shine on a project propels it from flat to fabulous.

You can add foil to a project surface anytime during construction. All you need is foil, an iron, and an adhesive—a liquid, a granulated product, or a fusible web all work. For a unique look, make a dimensional foil appliqué with stick glue and your glue gun.

Foil comes in a variety of colors and in holographic designs. It may be packaged either as an assortment of small sheets or in 1-yard (0.9 m) lengths. New sheets give solid, bright shine. When the sheets start to wear out, they get even better because you can use several colors in succession for a softer, more complex look.

materials and tools

Plastic cover for the table

Foam brush: 1" (2.5 cm)

Foil adhesive

Stamp: rubber, acrylic, wood, or foam, with a bold, deep design

Fabric

Foil: various colors

Iron

Fusible web: Wonder-Under Transfer Web

Cooking parchment
(available at grocery stores)

Granulated adhesive:
Bo-Nash 007 Bonding Agent

Glue gun

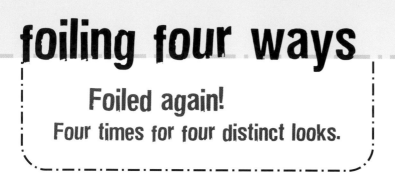

foiling four ways

Foiled again!
Four times for four distinct looks.

Preparation

Protect your work surface with the plastic cover. Before you begin, read through all of the techniques described in this section. One technique may contain a detailed instruction that is necessary for related techniques.

Direct to Fabric Foil Stamping

Brush foil adhesive onto the stamp. Try to get an even coat on the stamp but don't worry about a little excess on the edges. Stamp the adhesive onto your fabric and let it dry completely (two hours to overnight). Place a foil sheet over the dry adhesive, color side up. Set a dry iron to medium-high. Turn the iron slightly to its side and burnish the foil sheet three or four times with the edge. If the foil sheet starts to melt, turn the temperature down. Allow the foil to cool, then peel the sheet off the adhesive.

Shaped Foil

Cut a shape out of the fusible web. Iron the shape onto the fabric and remove the release paper. Place a foil sheet over the web, color side up, and burnish with the edge of the iron three or four times.

Note: Protect any previously applied foil from direct contact with the iron with parchment paper.

Star Dusting with Foil

Sprinkle granulated adhesive onto the fabric. Cover with a piece of parchment and iron until the granules melt onto the fabric. Remove the parchment, cover the melted granules with a foil sheet, color side up, and burnish with the edge of the iron. Protect all previously foiled areas with parchment.

Dimensional Foiling

Place a foil sheet, dull side up, on a heat-resistant ironing board. Heat a glue gun and then draw a shape with the glue on the foil sheet. Allow the glue to cool completely and then peel it off the foil. To attach the shape to fabric, place it glue side up on the ironing board. Place the fabric, wrong side up, over the shape and lightly press until the shape adheres to the fabric.

Susan Suggests

Hand-wash foiled fabrics; do not dry-clean.

fabric beads

Fabric beads make a fabulous closure on a garment, but think of using them in a necklace or on a wall hanging!

Place them in a pictorial piece as sculptural elements, as flower stems, as the parts of a chair, or as fence rails.

Discover how to create your own beads out of fabric that coordinates with your projects—without an expensive trip to the bead store.

Craft your beads in different shapes, decorate them with threads and trim or even other beads, foil them to add shine, and make them from fabrics that ravel in an interesting way. They are so quick and easy to create, you'll want to make lots.

Using the following method, you'll make sturdy beads that won't flatten out. If they will receive extra hard wear, coat them with polyurethane to seal them.

Sew finished beads to your background fabric or glue them down with permanent fabric adhesive.

materials and tools

Iron

Fusible web: Wonder-Under Transfer Web

Fabric: small pieces, include cotton batik and dupioni silk

Bamboo skewer

Decorative threads and yarns

Sponge brush: 1" (2.5 cm)

Foil adhesive

Foil: various colors

Sewing needle and thread

Permanent fabric adhesive: Fabri-Tac

fabric beads

Discover a quartet of ways
to create beautiful beads.

Preparation
Before you begin, read through all of the techniques described in this section. One technique may contain a detailed instruction that is necessary for related techniques.

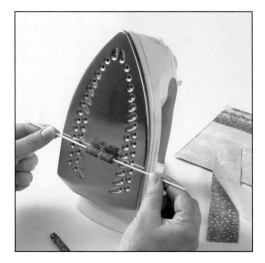

Cylinder Beads
Iron fusible web onto the back of fabric. Cut the fabric into strips that are the width of the bead you want, usually 1" to 1½" (2.5 to 3.8 cm) wide by 8" to 10" (20.3 to 25.4 cm) long. Remove the release paper from the fusible web and roll the fabric strip onto a bamboo skewer. Roll the skewered bead on an iron set to the proper temperature for the fabric, to fuse the fabric layers together. Don't roll too long, or you may fuse the bead onto the skewer permanently.

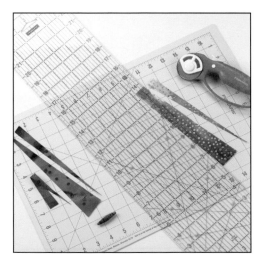

Tapered Beads
This technique works especially well with batik fabric or other hand-dyed fabrics that have scattered colors. Iron fusible web onto the back of fabric. Cut the fabric into strips as in "Cylinder Beads." Cut one end of each strip into a long, centered point. Remove the release paper from the fusible web and roll a strip onto the skewer, starting at the wide end. Melt the fabric layers together on the hot iron.

Decorative Touches

Decorate your beads with eyelet trim, thin yarn, narrow silk ribbon, or metallic thread. Lay the trim across one side of the bead. Wind it up the bead and back to the start of the trim. Tie the two ends together in a knot and let the tails dangle. Brush foil adhesive onto a bead and apply foil after it dries. (See "Direct to Fabric Foil Stamping" on page 18 for a description of this technique.)

Frayed Beads

To create a dupioni silk tapered bead, apply permanent fabric adhesive only to the pointed tip of the fabric, on the back side. This will secure the rolled layers, and the unglued edges will create an attractively raveled, soft bead. Think of all the possible variations!

Susan Suggests

Add further interest by wrapping a colored wire around your beads, or go for extra glitz by threading seed beads onto a wire and then wrapping the bead.

lasagna dyeing

This method, also called "painting silk layers," makes it fun and exciting to paint several pieces of silk at the same time.

You'll stack four or five layers of silk pieces and then paint the surface with a free-flowing textile paint. This very thin paint gives the effect of dyeing without the mess and chemicals. The paint sinks through the fabric layers and creates a vari-ety of patterns, depending on the absorbency and the position of the fabric in the stack. The colors blend together and always produce a surprise.

I painted my project pieces with magenta and turquoise and then applied golden yellow. Suddenly, orange, bright green, and yellow sprang to life.

Wait for all the layers to dry (the hardest part of all!), then peel them apart to reveal the wonderful results.

materials and tools

Plastic cover for the table

Silk in four or five weaves

Iron

Nozzle-tipped squeeze bottles, pipettes, or eyedroppers

Transparent fabric paint: Dye-na-Flow in magenta, turquoise, and golden yellow

White cotton fabric for the backing

Sheer fusible web: Misty-white Fuse

Cooking parchment (available at grocery stores)

Ribbon to cover edges

lasagna dyeing

Work step-by-step
into a surprise ending.

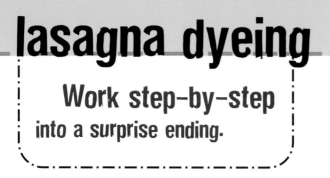

Preparation

Protect your work surface with the plastic cover.

1

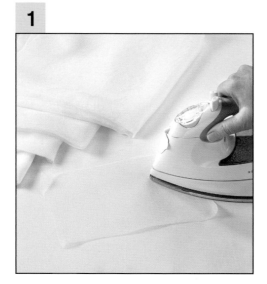

Cut four or five pieces of silk to the same size—6" to 9" (15.2 to 22.9 cm) squares work well. Set the iron to the temperature for silk and press to remove all wrinkles. Stack the pieces together. Do not pin them because the pin would attract the paint, and a little shifting is fine.

2

Fill two or three nozzle-tipped squeeze bottles, pipettes, or eyedroppers with separate colors of transparent paint, and create lines or patterns on the top layer of silk. Leave some white space as you work. The paint will flow freely as it dries, generating its own design.

Note: Avoid using colors opposite each other on the color wheel (red/green, blue/orange, purple/yellow) because they make muddy colors when mixed.

3

Peel the silk layers apart when they are dry. Notice how the pattern differs greatly depending on the weave of the silk and the position of the fabric in the stack. Press the pieces to set the paint.

4

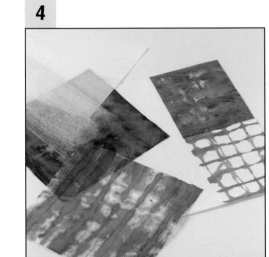

Cut a piece of cotton fabric the size you want for your finished project. Cover it with a layer of fusible web. Arrange the silk pieces into a pleasing composition, cover it with a piece of cooking parchment, and fuse. Sew or fuse the ribbon over the edges.

Susan Suggests

For the various silk weaves, choose netting, crinkle chiffon, patterned organza, and habotai. Look for silk fabrics with woven-in designs for extra impact.

monoprinting

Monoprinting is a tried and true printing method that produces one-of-a-kind freeform designs.

The process involves manipulating paints on a nonporous surface such as marble, glass, or hard plastic, then pressing fabric onto the paint and lifting to create the unique artwork.

You can make a wonderful print on two pieces of fabric and keep everything contained in a plastic sheet protector while you are working! It's like finger painting without touching the paint!

A metallic paint works beautifully for this method, and the prints can be done on black fabric for dramatic results. The finished prints will be mirror images of each other. The possibilities for vest fronts, coordinated purse panels, or interesting wall hangings are unlimited.

materials and tools

Plastic cover for the table

Plastic sheet protector
(available at office supply stores)

Metallic fabric paint:
Lumiere, two or three colors

Spoons or wooden craft sticks to use
with the paint

Fabric: black, approximately 9" x 12"
(22.9 x 30.5 cm)

monoprinting

A fun process that creates its own statement.

Preparation
Protect your work surface with the plastic cover.

1

Cut two edges off the sheet protector, leaving one connected edge. Open the sheet protector on the plastic-covered table. Shake or stir the paint thoroughly and spoon the paint onto one side of the plastic. Use two or three colors that coordinate with or complement each other.

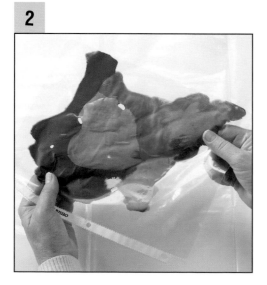

2

Close the sheet protector. Manipulate the paint by pushing with your fingers so paint covers most of the area inside the plastic. Work quickly so the paint does not bead up or start to dry. Open the sheet protector.

3

Place one piece of fabric on each side of the sheet protector, then close it. Quickly and *gently* rub both sides of the plastic to transfer the paint to the fabric. Do not push the paint into the grain of the fabric or the colors will appear dull.

4

Remove the fabric pieces from the sheet protector and separate them. Let them dry flat on the plastic-covered table for 24 hours. Heat set the paint with an iron set to the proper temperature for the fabric for 30 seconds on both sides of the fabric, or place the fabric in a hot dryer for 30 minutes.

Susan Suggests

You can use an 18" x 12" (45.7 x 30.5 cm) folded piece of fabric for a butterfly effect. Be very careful when placing the fabric within the sheet protector.

silk fusion

Silk fusion, also called silk paper, consists of silk fiber that has not been spun into yarn or thread.

A textile medium, used as a soft adhesive, holds the fibers together. You may want to experiment with different mediums depending on the degree of stiffness you want for your final fabric.

Bombyx silk, from silkworms that eat mulberry leaves, is light, almost white in color, and quite smooth. The silkworms that produce tussah silk eat oak leaves and their silk is gold-colored (although it's often bleached) and coarser than bombyx. Either works well for silk fusion.

Add a variety of decorative elements to your fusion, or cut up the sheet and include the pieces in wool felting for a beautiful, tactile play of texture on texture. Of course, beading or other embellishments on the finished silk fusion add a fun touch and are easy to attach to the firm surface.

Use your silk fusion for wall hangings, containers such as boxes and bowls, book covers, and clothing.

materials and tools

Plastic cover for the table

Tulle or netting

Silk roving: bombyx or tussah, two or three colors

Decorative elements: ribbon, skeleton or silk leaves, or Angelina fibers

Shampoo without conditioner

Mixing container

Bristle brush: 1" (2.5 cm)

Paper towels

Textile medium

Screen or plastic mesh

silk fusion

Follow each step, or **omit the embellishments** for another look.

Preparation

Protect your work surface with the plastic cover.

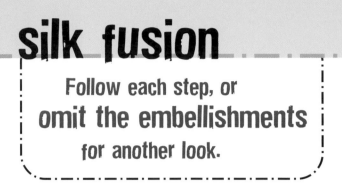

1

Lay out a piece of tulle or netting on your work surface. Pull small amounts of silk fiber from the hank of roving and lay them parallel to each other on half of the tulle in a thin and even layer.

Note: For the nicest look, never cut the silk roving. Hold your hands about 8" (20.3 cm) apart on the hank of roving and pull it apart.

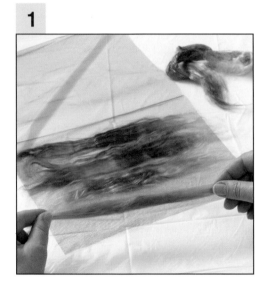

2

Lay additional fibers crosswise on top of the first layer. Lay a third layer of fibers in the direction of the first layer. Check for thin spots in the layers and fill in, if necessary.

3

Lay silk or skeleton leaves, ribbons, or other decorative elements on top of the third layer of fibers. Cover them with wisps of fibers to hold them in place. Fold the other half of the tulle over the top of the layered silk fibers and embellishments.

4

Dissolve about ½ teaspoon (2.5 ml) of shampoo into 2 cups (0.5 l) of water. Brush the solution on the tulle until all layers are thoroughly saturated. Blot out as much water as possible with paper towels. Coat both sides of the tulle with full-strength textile medium. Let the fusion dry on a screen or piece of plastic mesh and then peel it off the tulle.

Susan Suggests

Create thickness through additional layers. After completing a few projects, you will be able to judge how thick you want your silk fusion for its final use.

silk cocoons and more

Silk comes in wondrous forms, and now many of them are readily available to quilters and fabric artists.

No other fabric feels like silk or slurps color like silk.

Cocoons are the source of silk filament, and a dried worm is inside each one. Silk carrier rods are a by-product of the silk-making process and can be peeled into thin layers. Hankies are gossamer-thin layers of silk fiber that can be further peeled apart.

Use the cocoons, carrier rods, and hankies to make necklaces, tassels, and embellishments on wall hangings or for other creative projects.

materials and tools

Plastic cover for the table

Silk cocoons

Small scissors with a very sharp tip

Transparent fabric paint:
Dye-na-Flow, assorted colors

Container

Silk carrier rods

Hemostat or tweezers

Pipettes or eyedroppers

Paper towels

Silk hankies
(a form of silk, not a handkerchief)

Spray bottle containing water

Iron

Permanent fabric adhesive: Fabri-Tac

silk cocoons and more

Combine all three silk products on one fabric, or try each as a separate technique to enhance other projects.

Preparation

Protect your work surface with the plastic cover. Before you begin, read through all of the techniques described in this section. One technique may contain a detailed instruction that is necessary for related techniques.

Prepare the Cocoons

Cut from one end of the cocoon to the other with the scissors. Or, if you plan to make a tassel, cut off one end of the cocoon. With your fingers, gently pry open the cocoon and let the dried worm fall out. You can also leave the worm inside if you like.

Add Color to Cocoons and Carrier Rods

Pour enough transparent paint into a container to submerge the cocoons and rods. Use a hemostat or tweezers to handle the silk items. The silk cocoons and rods will be somewhat resistant to absorbing the paint. Soak them until they become covered with paint, but do not soak them longer than 10 minutes (especially if you've left the worm inside, as it may soften). Dribble one or two more colors over them with a pipette or eyedropper before they become paint saturated (adding additional colors will change the original color in the container). Remove the cocoons and rods from the paint and dry them on paper towels.

Freeform Hankie Painting

Carefully pour any paint remaining in the container onto a silk hankie. If the hankie resists the paint, spray it with water. Dribble other colors over the hankie with a pipette or eyedropper, but be careful to leave white spaces for the paint to bleed into. If the hankie is overly saturated, place a second, unpainted hankie on top of it and blot some of the paint. A bonus! Two hankies with coordinated colors. Allow the hankies to dry and then iron them for ease of handling.

Go Creative

Set your iron on silk and use steam to press the silk rods flat. The rods can be woven, used as stems for cocoon flowers, rolled and stuffed into cocoon openings, or used as they are.

The cocoons can be cut to form flower petals, made into beads, decorated and made into tassels, or cut in half and attached to a silk hankie with permanent fabric adhesive.

Use the hankies as backgrounds or stuff small bits of hankie into the ends of the cocoons for tassel embellishments.

Susan Suggests

Make a silk cocoon tassel! Cut off the end of two silk cocoons and remove the worms. Paint the cocoons two different colors. Let dry.

Snip the end of one cocoon into sharp points and slip it over the second cocoon. With thread and a sharp chenille or darning needle, poke into the cocoon on one side of the closed end and come out on the opposite side. Pull the thread through. Cut the thread and tie the ends together.

Decorate the cocoons with glitter, seed beads, or fancy threads. Slip a fancy yarn or part of a painted silk hankie into the open end of the tassel, if desired, and glue in place.

brayer painting

Brayers are like small versions of the rollers used to paint walls.

They are very useful for applying paint to fabric in a variety of ways—each one interesting and fun! You can create patterns by placing items around the roller before loading it with the paint. Brayers with a removable roller make it easy to wind threads and fibers around the roller. Create a different effect by putting objects under your fabric and rolling a paint-filled brayer over the top.

Creating garment fabric with abstract designs is easy, as the brayer covers a large area quickly. It is simple to create fascinating texture with common household items. Mix the techniques for a variety of looks. Let's get started!

materials and tools

Plastic cover for the table

Medium-bodied fabric paint:
Lumiere or Neopaque, assorted colors

Glass with taped edges or
an acrylic surface

Soft rubber brayer (not sponge) with a
removable roller

Fabric

Masking tape

Iron

Objects for texture: rubbing plates,
bamboo placemats, cheesecloth, produce
bags, bubble wrap, leaves, plastic doilies,
or scrapbook-type corrugated cardboard

String or rubber bands

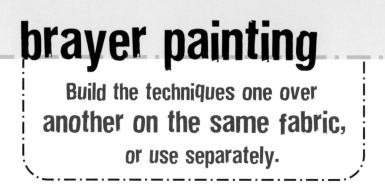

Build the techniques one over **another on the same fabric,** or use separately.

Preparation

Protect your work surface with the plastic cover. Before you begin, read through all of the techniques described in this section. One technique may contain a detailed instruction that is necessary for related techniques.

Load the Brayer

Pour a puddle of paint onto part of a sheet of glass or acrylic. Roll the brayer over the paint to spread it into an even layer. Roll the brayer on a clean spot on the glass, in one direction, to flatten any thick paint and evenly distribute paint around the roller. Press lightly when moving the roller.

Fashion a Plaid Pattern

Attach your fabric to the table with masking tape. Roll the paint-loaded brayer down a section of fabric to create a line. Note that every revolution of the roller removes a layer of paint from the brayer, so the color lightens rapidly across the fabric. Apply more paint to the brayer and paint another line. Load the brayer with a second color (no need to clean it), and roll over the fabric, perpendicular to the already painted lines, to create your plaid. The end result will be an interesting composition, depending on how quickly the roller runs out of paint, where the painted areas overlap, how evenly you loaded the brayer, and how smooth the plastic is under the fabric. Press to heat set the paint.

Work with Texture

Place your chosen texture object or objects under a piece of fabric. Roll over the top of the fabric with a loaded brayer. Reload the brayer when it runs out of paint. Notice how the roller will create a negative image when you go beyond the edge of the item underneath the fabric. Press to heat set the paint.

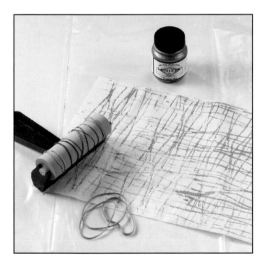

Design Stripes and Grids

Prepare an even layer of paint on the glass or acrylic. Clean the brayer. Remove the roller. Wind string or fibers around it or place rubber bands of varying widths on it. Replace the roller in the brayer and load it with paint. Roll over the fabric, either making irregular stripes by going in one direction or a grid by going in both directions. Press to heat set the paint.

Note: The paint on the glass or acrylic must be evenly rolled out so paint does not move into the spaces between the string or rubber bands.

Susan Suggests

Scatter rubber bands under a piece of fabric for an interesting abstract effect.

splash and puddle painting

Dye-na-Flow paint, a very thin paint that acts like a dye, flows over the surface of and mixes readily on fabric.

One of the advantages of using paint instead of dye is immediately seeing your colors blend and patterns develop. You'll have *no* control over what the paints do after you apply them to the fabric, which generates extra fun!

You'll quickly grasp color theory as you watch primary colors (red, yellow, blue) mix together to form secondary colors (purple, green, orange) and see complementary colors (see page 47) blend to make earth tones.

In this sample, the complementary colors purple and yellow formed brown when they bled into each other.

Try a piece of silk or pima cotton for this project, as these fabrics are easy to manipulate.

materials and tools

Plastic cover for the table

Fabric: China silk or silk twill (8 to 12 mm) or pima cotton

Transparent fabric paint: Dye-na-Flow, assorted colors

Pipettes or eyedroppers

Spray bottle containing water

Sponge brushes: 1" (2.5 cm)

Coarse salt

Iron

Bubble wrap

Heavy-duty aluminum foil

Masking tape

Note: Prepared for dyeing (PFD) fabric works best.

splash and puddle painting

Once you try the various techniques separately, **mix and match them** for spontaneous, interesting patterns.

Preparation

Protect your work surface with the plastic cover. Before you begin, read through all of the techniques described in this section. One technique may contain a detailed instruction that is necessary for related techniques.

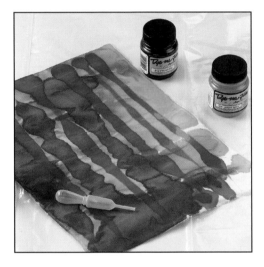

Create a Background

Lay a piece of fabric on your work surface. You will create this pattern using one or more colors, as desired. Dribble paint with a pipette or eyedropper across the fabric in parallel lines. Now dribble paint onto the fabric in lines that are perpendicular to the first lines. Leave some white space for the paint to flow into. After a couple of minutes, add more paint if you think there is too much white space, or spray the fabric with water to make the paint run.

Salt Patterning

Spray the fabric with water. Paint a random pattern over the entire surface with two or three colors, using a separate sponge brush for each color. Spray the fabric with more water to make the colors blend. Immediately sprinkle coarse salt over the surface. Let the fabric dry slowly to allow the salt to push the paint into fascinating configurations. Wrinkles in the plastic or ripples in the fabric will also form designs. After the fabric dries, brush off the salt, heat set the fabric with the iron or in a dryer for 30 minutes, then wash out any salt residue.

Bubble-Wrap Patterning

Lay a piece of bubble wrap on the table, bubble side up. Lay a piece of fabric over it and spray the fabric with water. Paint a random pattern over the entire surface of the fabric with one or more colors, using a separate sponge brush for each color. As you work, push the brush down into the valleys created by the bubble wrap. Spray the fabric with more water until you see distinct circle patterns. Allow the fabric to dry completely, then press to heat set the paint.

Color Pleating

Cut a piece of heavy-duty aluminum foil to the size of your fabric (a fat quarter, 18" x 22" [45.7 x 55.9 cm], or a smaller piece works well). Use masking tape to attach the ends of the fabric to the foil. Crease the foil and fabric together into 1" (2.5 cm) pleats. Unfold the pleats slightly. Place the pleated fabric and foil on your table. Spray the fabric with water. Using enough paint so the colors will be able to blend together on the sides of the mountains and in the valleys, apply a color with a sponge brush on the mountains. Using a separate sponge brush, apply another color in the valleys. After the paint dries, press the fabric flat, using a heat setting appropriate to the fabric, to reveal a wonderful soft stripe and to set the paint.

Susan Suggests

The color wheel can help guide you through color choices. Complementary colors are yellow/purple, blue/orange, and red/green. Here is an easy way to remember this: the complement of any primary color is the combination of the other two primary colors.

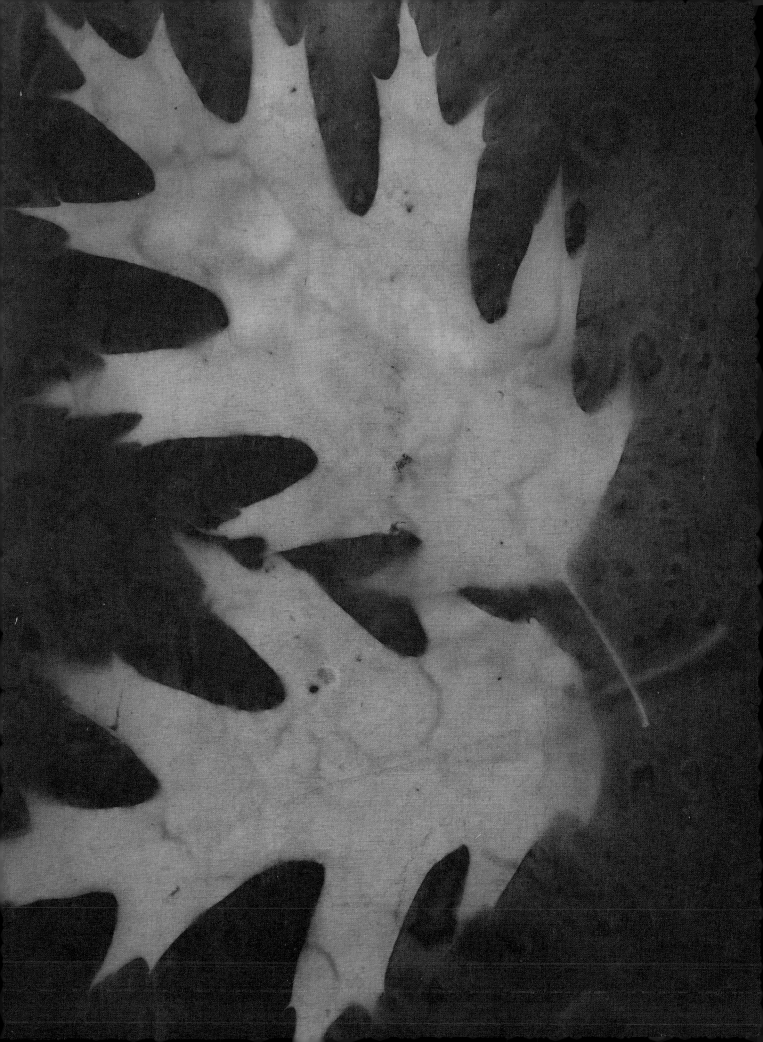

sunprinting with paint

Sunprinting is an exciting and delightfully simple technique that uses the sun to imprint images on cloth.

The entire surface of a fabric is painted, objects are arranged on it, and the fabric is dried in direct sunlight. The color under the objects lightens, but the brilliant color of the painted fabric exposed to the sun remains.

The intensity of the sun affects the quality of the prints, so plan ahead and have your materials ready for when the weather cooperates. Make sun blocks from items found around the house and yard. Each will make a distinct pattern. If the day is breezy, weigh down your objects with small stones or tape netting over them. Do not use glass or another solid cover because it will prevent the paint from drying and printing your image.

materials and tools

Plastic cover for the table

Fabric: light-colored, flat, and wrinkle-free

Foam core or plywood: plastic-covered

Spray bottle containing water

Transparent fabric paint: Dye-na-Flow

Sponge brush: 1" (2.5 cm)

Sun blocks: leaves, rice, macaroni, torn cheesecloth, or plastic letters

Small stones, glass marbles, or netting (optional)

Iron

sunprinting with paint

A quick and easy process **that creates looks from** sophisticated to whimsical.

Preparation
Protect your work surface with the plastic cover.

1

Place the fabric on a plastic-covered board. Any threads lying on the surface of the fabric or the board will create a print and so will folds or wrinkles in the plastic. Spray the fabric with water until damp.

2

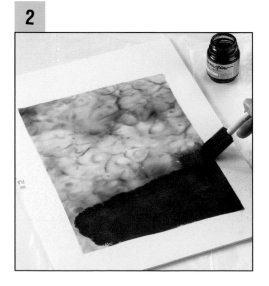

Paint the entire surface of the damp fabric with paint using a sponge brush. Take the paint straight out of the bottle. Work quickly so the paint stays wet, as dry paint will not print.

3

Place your sun blocks on top of the fabric. Spray the fabric with water again and press the edges of the objects firmly into the wet paint. They must lie flat; edges that are not flat against the fabric allow sun underneath and you will not get a clear, sharp print. Weigh down the objects, if necessary, with small stones or glass marbles, or tape a piece of netting over the project if the weather is breezy. The netting will print, but that adds an interesting secondary design. Place the project in direct sunlight.

4

When the fabric has dried completely, remove the objects. Heat set the paint by ironing the fabric for three minutes or placing it in a hot dryer for 30 minutes. Be sure to look at the back of the fabric—sometimes it is as pretty as the front!

Susan Suggests

Try layering your sunprints. After printing and drying your fabric, repaint with another color and use the same or different objects to print the fabric for a luscious layered effect.

sponge painting

Sponge painting is a quick and easy technique for creating textured patterns and backgrounds.

Small pieces of nonhardening sponge work well with medium-bodied fabric paints, and you can paint on wet or dry fabric to achieve different effects. Look for sponges that have holes of various sizes, and buy several so you always have a dry sponge ready for the next application. Use a transparent paint to fill in the background areas after the first sponge painting is dry.

materials and tools

Plastic cover for the table

Scissors

Freezer paper for palette and stencils

Iron

Stencil fabric: solid color

Acrylic stencils

Hydrophilic sponges:
yellow with rounded edges
(available at hobby stores or paint stores)

Metallic fabric paint: Lumiere

Background fabric

Medium-bodied, transparent fabric paint:
Textile Colors

Sea sponges
(available at wallpaper and paint stores)

Sheer fusible web: Misty-white Fuse

sponge painting

Sponging and stenciling combine for a textural treat.

Preparation

Protect your work surface with the plastic cover.

1

Cut a stencil out of freezer paper and iron the freezer paper to the stencil fabric. You can also use a pre-cut acrylic stencil. Cut the hydrophilic sponges into small, easy-to-hold pieces. Pour metallic paint onto a freezer-paper palette. Dip a sponge into the paint and then dab the sponge onto the freezer paper to remove the excess (don't go directly to the fabric or the sponge texture will not show on the first application).

2

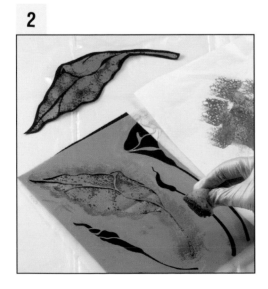

Dab the paint on the fabric through the stencil openings. The less paint you have on the sponge, the more textured the design will look. Rinse the sponge and let the paint dry.

3

Create color movement and texture on the background fabric with another piece of sponge and the medium-bodied, transparent paint. Refill the sponge with paint as necessary. Devise your own pattern or follow the print on the fabric, if any. Use a variety of paint colors, if you wish. Try layering colors by dabbing a second color alongside of, and slightly overlapping, the first color. Allow the paint to dry.

4

Unify your color scheme by sponging transparent paint in a complementary color (see page 47) over the fabric using the sea sponge. Rinse your sponges in water to clean. Heat set the paint by ironing the fabric for three minutes or placing it in a hot dryer for 30 minutes.

Cut around the stenciled motif leaving a border of stencil fabric. This will ground the appliqué when it's fused to the background fabric. Attach the appliqué to the background fabric with fusible web.

Note: Stencil by Diane Ericson (see Resources).

Susan Suggests

If you like a watercolor look, spray the fabric with water either before or after painting with the fabric paint.

Earth Whispers

The earth whispers to every listening ear...
through leaves, grass, wind, and rain.
Peace found in things always here,
Wisdom found in ageless forms,
New life springing forth again and again.
Do you hear?

image to fabric sheet transfer

Transferring your favorite photographs to fabric is very fast and easy.

Printable fabric sheets are available in cotton and silk and even in silk organza for transparent layering. The sheets vary in price, but all work the same way—the main difference is their washability. If you want your project to be washable, test-wash and dry a sheet of the product you choose.

With your computer printer, a scanner, or an inexpensive color copier, fabric can be printed with digital photos, scanned children's artwork, photocopied real-life objects, or images sent to you by e-mail.

Then enjoy creating lovely items with your personally printed fabric. Scatter fabric-printed flower images among other pieces of a patchwork quilt, blend a printed landscape scene into a pieced or appliquéd frame, or put your own face onto an art doll to reveal your hidden persona!

materials and tools

Plain, white paper

Computer printer, scanner, and/or color copier

Objects to place on the copier: flowers, leaves, or children's artwork

Printed images or word-processed documents

Prepared fabric sheets for inkjet printing or photocopying

Sheer fusible web: Misty-white Fuse

Cooking parchment (available at grocery stores) or press sheet

Iron

image to fabric sheet transfer

Print words or images onto **treated fabric using your** ink-jet printer or copier.

Preparation

Before you begin, read through all of the techniques described in this section. One technique may contain a detailed instruction that is necessary for related techniques.

Preparing to Scan or Copy

As some machines print on the top and some on bottom side of the paper, draw an X on a test sheet of plain paper and put it through the copier or printer to determine which way to feed the fabric sheets. Collect all the materials needed to compose an image to scan or copy. If you want separate images of flowers or family photographs, arrange small ones on the copier or scanner so you can copy or print three or four images on one fabric sheet. To easily create a collage of items, compose and adhere them to a piece of paper and then place it face down on the scanner or copier.

Words Over Images

Print or copy a full-color image to a cotton fabric sheet and a poem or other writing to a transparent organza fabric sheet. Your image will remain bright even though it will be beneath the organza.

Images Over Words

Print or copy a poem or other writing to a cotton fabric sheet and a full-color image to a transparent organza fabric sheet. The words will still be distinct and the image will become muted and subtle.

Finishing

Cut a piece of fusible web to the size of your fabric sheets. Place the web over the cotton sheet and then place the organza sheet on top. Cover with parchment or a press sheet and fuse the three layers together using an iron.

Susan Suggests

Try printing black-and-white clip art on a fabric sheet and tinting the art with fabric paints before fusing organza over it.

painted fusible web

Fabric artists have adapted fusible web—which once simply hid between layers of fabric—into an art element.

This fine web of fusible adhesive can be painted and then used as an overlay, a background, or an appliqué.

Using a thin fabric paint to add color to the web while it remains on its paper backing causes the paper to crinkle, which adds pattern to the web. The decorative web can then be fused onto a piece of printed or solid-color fabric.

This technique is perfect for people who like serendipity in the final product because the web often releases from the paper backing unevenly.

materials and tools

Plastic cover for the table

Fusible web: Wonder-Under Transfer Web

Transparent fabric paint:
Dye-na-Flow, assorted colors

Sponge brushes: 1" (2.5 cm)

Hair dryer (optional)

Background fabric: high color contrast,
such as black and white

Iron

Cooking parchment
(available at grocery stores)

Appliqué fabric: large motif

Granulated adhesive:
Bo-Nash 007 Bonding Agent

painted fusible web

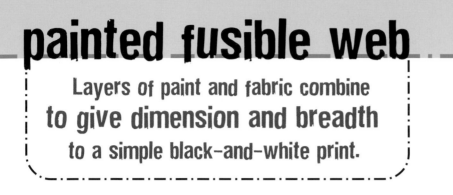

Layers of paint and fabric combine **to give dimension and breadth** to a simple black-and-white print.

Preparation
Protect your work surface with the plastic cover.

1

Lay a piece of fusible web on the table, web side up. Cover the web with transparent paint, working quickly. Apply as many colors as you like, using a separate brush for each color. You may add water to the paint if you want a diffused effect. The paper backing will crinkle when it gets wet enough, so do not rework an area or you will flatten out the texture. Let the paint dry or speed up the process with a hair dryer.

2

Cut a piece of completely dry, painted fusible web to your chosen size. Place it web side down on the front of your background fabric, and iron over the paper backing for a few seconds. Make sure the edges are secure. Let cool and then peel the paper backing off of the web. Some areas of the web may stay on the paper backing, but that is part of the fun of this technique. Cover the fabric with parchment and press the web thoroughly into the fabric.

3

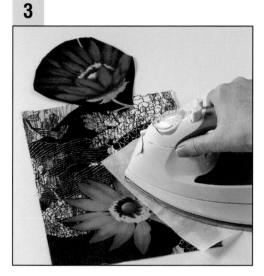

Cut a motif from the appliqué fabric. Place it on the background fabric. Protect all exposed web with parchment and press the appliqué thoroughly until it is secure.

Note: If an area under the appliqué lacks fusible web, sprinkle a little bonding agent on the fabric before heat setting.

4

Cut a second piece of painted web (perhaps a piece that reflects a color from the appliqué) and iron it over the motif, being careful to protect any exposed web with parchment. Cover the motif completely or partially, as you prefer. Peel off the paper backing, cover with parchment, and press the web thoroughly into the fabric.

Susan Suggests

Once the painted web is ironed to the fabric, you can further embellish it with foil, ribbons, or other fibers because it still has adhesive properties.

gossamer silk

Gossamer silk, unlike the stiffer silk fusion, remains soft and more like a fabric.

It can be used for scarves, vests, wall hangings, or fluttery window coverings. Gossamer silk is fairly sturdy because the sewing holds it together. It can be embellished either during the layering and sewing process or after the stabilizer is removed. Yarn, trim, or shapes cut from China silk, Angelina, or Mylar are just a few of the embellishments you can include as you lay out the fibers—just make sure your additions can withstand a bath in warm water. A bit of patience is needed when spreading out the silk and for stitching, but the results will get rave reviews.

materials and tools

Water-soluble stabilizer: Sulky Super Solvy

Hank of dyed silk top*

Embellishments: yarn, trim, or shapes of China silk, Angelina, or Mylar

Straight pins

Walking foot

Cotton thread to match the silk fiber

Sewing machine

Container of warm water to dissolve stabilizer

Paper towels or a terry towel

* This is processed silk fiber before it is spun into thread. Either tussah or bombyx silk will work.

gossamer silk

You'll work with soft silk fibers and embellishments **to create an interesting fabric** with a grid pattern in just four easy steps.

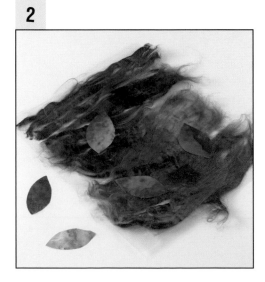

Lay out a piece of water-soluble stabilizer slightly larger than the size of the project you have planned. Pull apart (do not cut) the silk top, holding your hands about 8" (20.3 cm) apart on the hank and pulling.

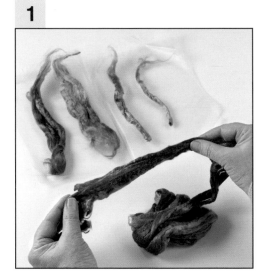

Carefully lay out thin strands of the silk fiber on the stabilizer, making sure there are no thick clumps and that the stabilizer is covered completely. Place embellishments on top of the fibers. Add more silk, if you like, or leave the additions to be caught by the stitching.

3

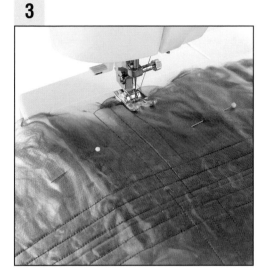

Cover the silk fiber with another piece of stabilizer and pin through all of the layers to hold the fibers and embellishments in place. Using a walking foot if you have one and cotton thread that matches the silk fiber, stitch through the layers in a ½" (1.3 cm) grid, starting with the horizontal and vertical lines in the middle (which will help hold everything in place while you do the rest of the stitching). Stitch the entire piece. It is not necessary to sew the stitching lines perfectly straight.

4

Soak the stitched piece in warm water for 5 to 10 minutes to dissolve the stabilizer. If you still feel stabilizer on the wet fabric or if the fabric is stiff after it dries, rinse it again. Spread the fabric out on paper towels or a terry towel, reshaping it to its original size. Let dry.

Note: Silk fiber dyed by Diane Bartels (see Resources).

Susan Suggests

Try free-motion sewing for an organic look, making sure your stitching lines cross over each other to create a net of stitches. Be sure to start stitching in the center of your composition.

resisting paint

You can control where paint flows over fabric or where it remains after it's applied.

Numerous intriguing methods, some mechanical and some chemical block paint from certain areas of the fabric. Each is called a "resist." Mechanical resists range from the fine hand-stitching of Japanese shibori to clothespins clamped on folds in the fabric. Chemical resists like gutta allow you to paint lovely florals or other images with precision. Potato dextrin dries on a fabric and forms a network of fine cracks that allows paint or dye to seep into them. For this project, simple school glue was used as a chemical resist and then washed out.

Try the methods shown here for quick, dramatic results. Different paint viscosities (consistencies) provide different results, so play with several to see what works best. As always, heat set the paint after it dries to make it permanent.

materials and tools

Plastic cover for the table	Container of warm water to dissolve glue
Fabric: white, preferably PFD	Toothbrush
Glue: Elmer's Washable School Glue Gel (the blue kind)	Masking tape, stickers, or adhesive shelf paper
Medium-bodied fabric paint: Textile Colors	String
Sponge brushes: 1" (2.5 cm)	Transparent fabric paint: Dye-na-Flow
Spray bottle containing water	Scissors
Iron	Rubber bands

resisting paint

Block the paint from the fabric or change **the way it flows across it.** These four techniques open a world of possibilities.

Preparation

Protect your work surface with the plastic cover. Before you begin, read through all of the techniques described in this section. One technique may contain a detailed instruction that is necessary for related techniques.

Glue Resist

Create a pattern on the fabric with the glue. Let the glue dry completely. Paint the fabric with the medium-bodied paint, using a sponge brush. Spray the painted fabric lightly with water if you would like the colors to blend. After the paint dries for 24 hours, heat set it on the wrong side of the fabric with a dry iron. Soak the fabric to soften the glue and then hand wash using a toothbrush to help remove the glue. Where the glue drawings covered the fabric, the original color will appear.

Tape Resist

Tear pieces of masking tape into strips and press them firmly onto the surface of the fabric, either randomly or in patterns. You can also use stickers or shelf paper cut into shapes. Paint over the resists with a sponge brush and the medium-bodied paint. Allow the paint to dry and then remove the resists. Take your design one step further by washing diluted paint over the painted piece to color the white areas and alter the color of the painted areas. Heat set the paint by ironing the fabric for three minutes or placing it in a hot dryer for 30 minutes.

String-Tied Patterning

Place a piece of string diagonally on a piece of dampened fabric. Drape the fabric over the string diagonally, forming two triangles. Hold the ends of the string and twirl the fabric until it is wound around the string. Scrunch the fabric together in the middle of the string and tie the string ends together. Dab thinned transparent paint into the wrinkles of the fabric with a sponge brush. The more paint you dab, the fewer white areas will remain. Let the fabric sit for 15 minutes or longer. Cut the string and unfold the fabric. Heat set the paint when dry.

Rubber Banding

Pick up a piece of dampened fabric from the center. Secure rubber bands around two or more sections about 1½" (3.8 cm) apart. Dab one or both types of paint into the folds with a sponge brush, using plenty of paint. The transparent paint will bleed between sections and the medium-bodied paint will be more contained by the rubber band resist. Let the fabric sit for 15 minutes or longer. Cut the rubber bands and unfold the fabric. Heat set the paint when dry.

Susan Suggests

Combine one or more of the techniques used in Resisting Paint with one or more techniques from Color Discharge with Bleach for myriad design options.

stamping with found objects

Rubber-stamping has been popular for years, but imagine other ways to stamp designs onto fabric.

Look around the house for common objects that could make unique prints. Check out your button box, desk, kitchen drawers, and workbench for items with interesting texture or items that can be carved or manipulated into patterns. A medium-bodied or a metallic paint works well for stamping because both retain the sharp edges you want. The key to making clear impressions with any stamping device is to load the stamp with enough paint to make a clear image, but not so much that the paint flows into the stamp's negative spaces. Work quickly when using fabric paint so it does not dry on the stamp.

materials and tools

Plastic cover for the table	Styrofoam trays
Glue for plastic: Goop	Ballpoint pen or toothpick
Buttons with flat contours and deep cuts	Sponge brush: 1" (2.5 cm)
Pill bottles or film canisters	Plexiglas and cardboard scraps
Spoon	Bubble wrap
Metallic fabric paint: Lumiere	String
Freezer paper or acrylic for a palette	Duct tape
Rubber brayer	Craft knife to carve erasers
Fabric	White erasers
Iron	Weather stripping

stamping with found objects

Fun stamping techniques to use together or solo.

Preparation

Protect your work surface with the plastic cover. Before you begin, read through all of the techniques described in this section. One technique may contain a detailed instruction that is necessary for related techniques.

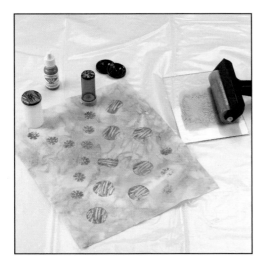

Button Stamping

Glue a button to the lid of an old pill bottle or film canister. Spoon paint onto your palette and smooth it out with the rubber brayer. Dip the button into the paint, then stamp the fabric. To keep the image distinct, load the stamp with paint each time you use it. For varied brightness, stamp two or three times before reloading with paint. Heat set the paint by ironing the fabric for three minutes or placing it in a hot dryer for 30 minutes.

Incised Styrofoam Stamping

Cut a rectangle from a Styrofoam tray. With a ballpoint pen or toothpick, draw several lines in the foam. Dab, don't brush, paint on the foam surface with a sponge brush (dabbing allows you to apply more paint). Turn the foam carved-side down on the fabric and rub the back of the foam to transfer the paint to the fabric. Do a test print before stamping your project because the foam will hold more paint the second time you use it. Heat set the paint when dry.

String and Bubble-Wrap Stamping

Wrap a Plexiglas or cardboard scrap with bubble wrap and another with string. Secure the bubble wrap in place on the back and form a handle with the duct tape. Spoon paint onto your palette and smooth it out with the rubber brayer. Dip the bubble wrap stamp into the paint, then stamp the fabric. Hold the string-wrapped stamp by one of the strings on the back and dip the front into the paint. Stamp the fabric. Heat set the paint when dry.

Carved-Eraser Stamping

Carve the erasers into your own one-of-a-kind designs and cut the weather stripping into shapes. Glue them separately or in a pattern to the Plexiglas scraps. Spoon paint onto your palette and smooth it out with the rubber brayer. Dip the stamps into the paint, then stamp the fabric. Heat set the paint when dry.

Note: Carved-eraser and weather-stripping stamps created by Diane Bartels.

Susan Suggests

Use an old toothbrush to clean out crevices if they clog while you're working.

color discharge with bleach

It is just as much fun to take the color out of fabric as to put it in!

Simple techniques for applying bleach to black or dark-colored fabric give you dramatic results. Be sure your fabrics are cotton or rayon, as bleach will dissolve silk. Doing a few swatches on various black fabrics before you start will determine what colors you will get. Different fabrics give surprisingly different shades of brown, tan, red, and green. You will need to work in a well-ventilated area, label your bottles and buckets, neutralize the bleach in the discharged fabrics, and wear rubber gloves when using liquid bleach. Do not use bleach if you have breathing problems or are pregnant.

materials and tools

Plastic cover for the table	Iron
Neutralizing powder: Anti-Chlor	Freezer paper
Water	Clorox Bleach Pen Gel
Bucket or small basin	Stencil (optional)
Fabric: cotton or rayon, black	Sun Light dishwasher gel
Cheesecloth	Acrylic scrap for a palette
Spray bottle	Rubber brayer or wooden paint mixing stick
Liquid bleach, fresh bottle	
Rubber gloves	Stamps: rubber or foam, with simple, bold designs
Lightweight cardboard	

color discharge with bleach

A variety of bleaching products and application methods offer myriad variations for discharging, or removing color.

Preparation

Protect your work surface with the plastic cover. Before proceeding with any of the steps, prepare the neutralizing solution so you can stop the bleaching action immediately when your fabric attains the color you want. Mix a tablespoon (15 ml) of Anti-Chlor per gallon (4 l) of water. Before you begin, read through all of the techniques described in this section. One technique may contain a detailed instruction that is necessary for related techniques.

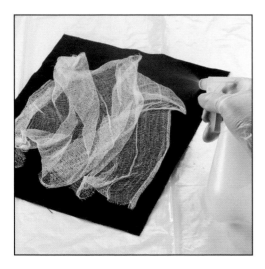

Misted Abstract Motifs

Lay the fabric on the table. Drape the cheesecloth on top of the fabric, creating creases and uneven edges. Use your hand to flatten the cheesecloth into the fabric. Fill the spray bottle with one part bleach and one part water. Spray over the cheesecloth and allow the fabric to rest until the color has changed around the edges. Don the rubber gloves and submerge the fabric and cheesecloth in the bucket of neutralizing solution to stop the bleaching action.

Designs with an Edge

Tear the edge of the cardboard into a wavy design. Place the torn edge near the top of the fabric and spray bleach water along the cardboard. Move the cardboard and spray along its edge again. Repeat until you get to the bottom of the fabric. Let the bleach work until you like the color, then don the rubber gloves and submerge the fabric in the bucket of neutralizing solution to stop the bleaching action.

Doodle Bleaching

Iron freezer paper, shiny side down, to the back of the fabric. This will stabilize it while you draw designs with a bleach pen. You can use a stencil, write words, or make abstract lines. Make sure you keep consistent pressure on the pen to avoid getting "exploding bubbles" in the stream of gel. Let the gel work until you like the color. Remove the freezer paper, don the rubber gloves, and submerge the fabric in the bucket of neutralizing solution to stop the bleaching action.

Gel Stamping

Pour dishwasher gel onto your palette and smooth it out with the brayer or wooden stick. Dab a foam or rubber stamp into the gel, then stamp the fabric. Let the gel work until you like the color, then don the rubber gloves and submerge the fabric in the bucket of neutralizing solution to stop the bleaching action.

Finishing

After the bleach is neutralized, wash the fabric in warm, soapy water and rinse.

Susan Suggests

When deciding when to neutralize your bleached pieces, remember that colors look darker on wet fabrics.

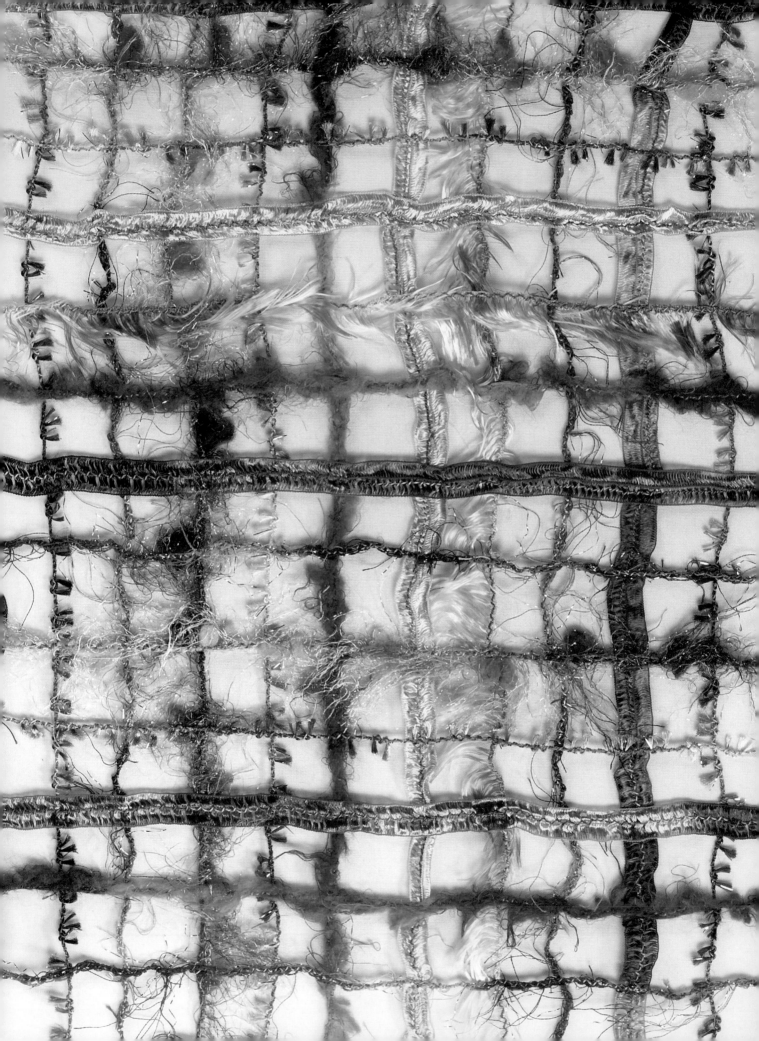

ribbon netting

Take advantage of the gorgeous trim, ribbon, and yarn available today and create a work of art.

Stitch a delicate, airy network of colorful, textural fibers to make a chic accessory or quick gift. Sew the ribbon netting to fabric to add a textural aspect, or use the trim to make an impressive wall hanging. Start with a water-soluble stabilizer, sew the trim or ribbon to it, and then dissolve the stabilizer away. You may find this addictive!

materials and tools

Water-soluble stabilizer: Sulky Super Solvy

Washable ribbon

Cotton thread: 40 or 50 weight

Sewing machine

Permanent marker (optional)

Straight pins

Container with water to dissolve stabilizer

Terry towel

ribbon netting

Grab your favorite ribbon and trim and in just a few **short steps, construct a colorful scarf or** a work of art...or maybe they're one and the same!

1

Cut two pieces of stabilizer slightly larger than the planned size of your finished project. Cut several pieces of ribbon the length of the stabilizer.

2

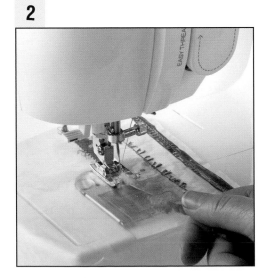

Place a ribbon parallel to the edge of one piece of stabilizer. Sew down the middle of the ribbon with a narrow zigzag stitch, backstitching the ends. Continue to add ribbons, spacing them about 1" (2.5 cm) apart, until the stabilizer is covered. The ribbons do not need to be perfectly straight, but draw guidelines on the stabilizer with a permanent marker, if you like.

3

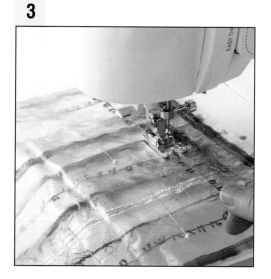

Lay the second piece of stabilizer on top of the first piece and pin in place. Sew additional ribbons perpendicular to those forming the first layer and backstitch at the ends.

4

Soak the piece in warm water to dissolve the stabilizer. If you feel any stickiness, soak again in clean water. Any remaining stabilizer will make the netting stiff. Reshape on a terry towel to dry.

Susan Suggests

Make a scarf using the netting technique. Cut a 20" x 60" (50.8 x 152.4 cm) piece of stabilizer. Cut eight to twelve pieces of ribbon 72" (183 cm) long. Sew the ribbons lengthwise over one-half of the stabilizer, letting an extra 6" (15.2 cm) hang off both ends to form fringe. Fold the stabilizer over the ribbons. Cut approximately 60 pieces of ribbon 10" (25.4 cm) long and sew them perpendicular to those forming the first layer, and backstitch at the ends. Dissolve the stabilizer.

nature printing

Flowers and leaves delight us during the growing season and are always nice to have around the rest of year.

Print and paint fabrics using natural materials, and you will enjoy the beauty of nature on wall hangings, quilts, household items, and clothing. Collect leaves and flowers any time of the year, press them between the pages of a thick phone book until they're dry, and then store them in plastic page protectors for future use. Simple flowers and leaves work best for printing and some will last through multiple uses.

materials and tools

Plastic cover for the table

Leaves

Phone book or other heavy book for pressing

Transparent fabric paint: Dye-na-Flow

Small spray bottle

Fabric

Newspaper

Sponge brushes: 1" (2.5 cm)

Opaque fabric paint: Neopaque, two or more colors

Rubber brayer

Metallic fabric paint: Lumiere

Iron

nature printing

Spray, brayer, accent—
three techniques to use alone
or to layer for autumnal bounty!

Preparation

Protect your work surface with the plastic cover. Press your leaves flat in a phone book or other heavy book for at least 20 minutes before use.

Spray

Pour the transparent paint into a small spray bottle. To produce a bold effect, use full-strength paint or for a softer look, dilute it with water. Place a large leaf on the fabric and spray the paint around the edges. Let the paint dry. Press with an iron to heat set when you complete your final Nature Printing technique.

Brayer: Preparation

Draw an outline the size of your journal page on the newspaper. Arrange the leaves inside the outline, vein-side (backside) up. Veining is more prominent on the back of leaves and offers a sharper image than you would get from the front. Remove the leaves one at a time from the newspaper, paint the backs with sponge brushes and two or more colors of opaque paint, and replace them in the design. Using variations of paint colors imitates the dappled hue of real leaves.

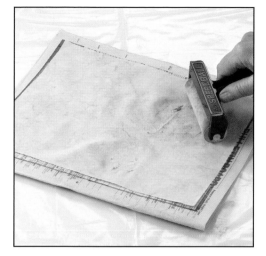

Brayer: Technique

Place a piece of fabric right side down over the leaves. Roll the brayer over it to transfer the paint to the fabric. Work quickly before the paint dries. This technique takes practice, so do several pieces and choose the best for your project. Peel the leaves off of the fabric and wipe them off if you want to use them again. Let the paint on the fabric dry for a few minutes.

Accent

To add an accent, spread metallic paint on another leaf, place it paint side down in the design, and brayer over it to transfer the paint to the fabric. Heat set the fabric with an iron when completely dry.

Susan Suggests

After your images are printed, dried, and heat set, they can be outlined with a permanent black marker or highlighted with stitching.

printout to fabric transfer

Who knew we would be using so much modern technology to create art?

If you have access to a laser or inkjet printer and an inkjet copier, you have the ability to print words and images on fabric without the expense of photo-transfer fabric sheets. When you use the one-step transfer method, you get a very subtle image. The inkjet and gel medium method is bolder—but messier! Sometimes painting over a transfer may smear some inkjet inks, so do a test run if neatness is a concern. For both methods, you can use a colored fabric.

materials and tools

Plastic cover for the table

Copyright-free images

Laser printer

Plain, white paper

Fabric: smooth-surfaced, white or light-colored

Iron

Inkjet printer or copier

Inkjet printer transparency sheet

Bristle brush with stiff, fine bristles

Gel medium: Golden Artist Colors Gel Mediums Regular Gel, matte

printout to fabric transfer

Quickly transfer an image with a laser printout, or use the equally quick three-step method using gel medium.

Preparation

Protect your work surface with the plastic cover. Before you begin, read through all of the techniques described in this section. One technique may contain a detailed instruction that is necessary for related techniques.

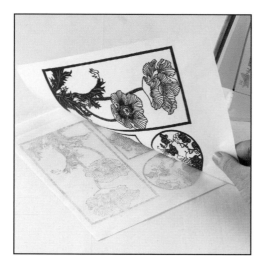

One-Step Laser Print Transfer

Make a black-and-white laser printout on plain paper. Turn it face down on white or light-colored fabric and iron the back of the paper for a couple of minutes on a hard surface. Lift a corner to check if the toner has transferred to the fabric. When it's ready, peel the paper off the fabric.

Inkjet Print an Image

Make an inkjet image on the rough side of a transparency sheet; both color and black-and-white images work well. If you don't know how the paper feeds into your printer or copier, draw an X on one side of a piece of paper and run it through to check. You can put several images on one sheet of transparency and then cut them apart.

Apply Gel Medium

Brush gel medium quickly and evenly, in both directions, onto the fabric. Extend the coverage slightly beyond the area the printed image will cover. Avoid getting the fabric too wet or the transparency will slide around and smear.

Transfer the Image

Place the transparency face down on the wet gel medium. Burnish the image with your fingernail, using circular strokes and pressing firmly. Make sure you burnish all areas. Lift a corner of the transparency to see if the image has transferred fully, and then slowly lift the transparency off the fabric. The image may not be perfect, especially if you missed an area when rubbing, but I like the "antiqued" look better anyway.

Note: Dover books are a very good source for copyright-free designs. Printed images are from *Authentic Chinese Cut-Paper Designs*, edited by Carol Belanger Grafton, part of the Dover Design Library.

Susan Suggests

If you want a darker laser-printed image, go to a copy shop and ask them to make a copy or printout using extra toner.

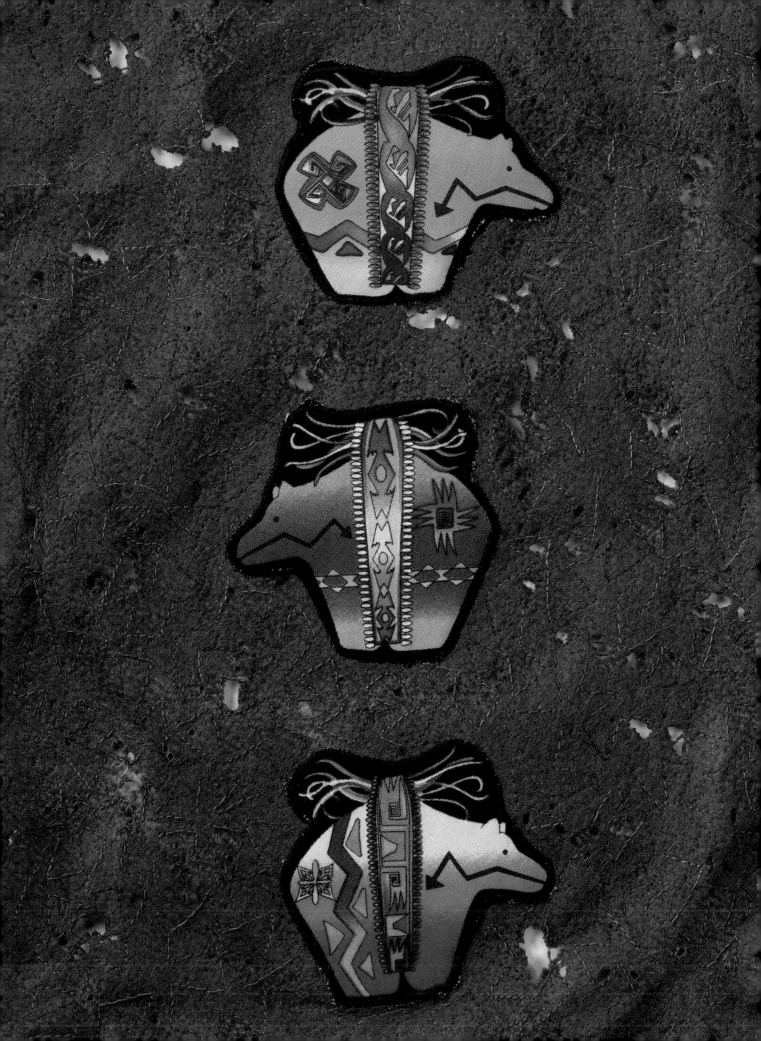

distressed felt

For those who are *really* adventurous, there are techniques in which you apply heat to fabrics to burn, melt, or distort them.

Soldering irons, changeable-tip heat tools, heat guns, regular irons, and hair dryers all are being used to alter fabric. Cotton or silk fabric that is applied to a synthetic fabric creates areas of resistance to the heat. You can also build up heavy concentrations of thread. On this project, synthetic felt was used with cotton appliqués and thread, and then a heat gun was used to melt and distress the felt creating holes and discolorations as well as shrinkage in the overall piece. Remember to do this outside or with proper ventilation, as the process will create fumes.

materials and tools

Iron

Fusible web: Wonder-Under Transfer Web

Fabric: cotton, with motifs

Synthetic felt: 9" x 12" (22.9 x 30.5 cm)

Sewing machine with satin stitch and darning feet

Cotton thread: matching and decorative

Heat gun

distressed felt

"Holey" moly! Heat and felt and fanciful fabric **turn into a lacy decorative accent** when put together in a few easy stages.

Iron fusible web to the back of the printed fabric, following the manufacturer's instructions. Cut out two or three motifs, leaving a generous ⅛" (3 mm) around the edge of each design.

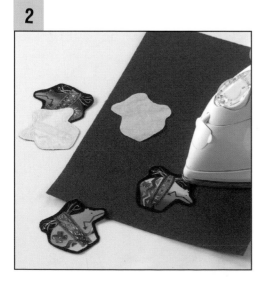

Peel off the paper backing from the cutouts and fuse the motifs to synthetic felt. Do not worry if the felt starts to shrink from the heat of the iron.

3

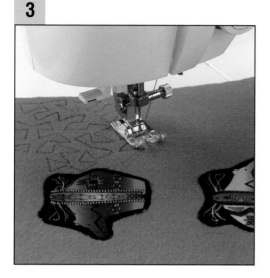

Satin stitch around the printed motifs with matching cotton thread. Set the machine for free motion stitching, drop the feed dogs, and change to decorative cotton thread. Stitch all over the background, using either a standard stippling design, triangular stippling like the sample, or loops. The stitching will hold the piece together when you melt the felt away.

4

Turn the piece over and heat over the entire piece with a heat gun held about 2" (5.1 cm) above the surface. The felt will start to shrink and discolor slightly. Keep heating the felt until holes start to appear. Turn the piece right side up and heat some more, trying to get holes and discoloration evenly spaced around the surface. You decide when the piece is finished—some people have hardly any felt left when they are done!

Susan Suggests

If you want significant changes in the character of your textile, use synthetic fabrics. Natural fibers tend to create ash when burned instead of melting or distorting.

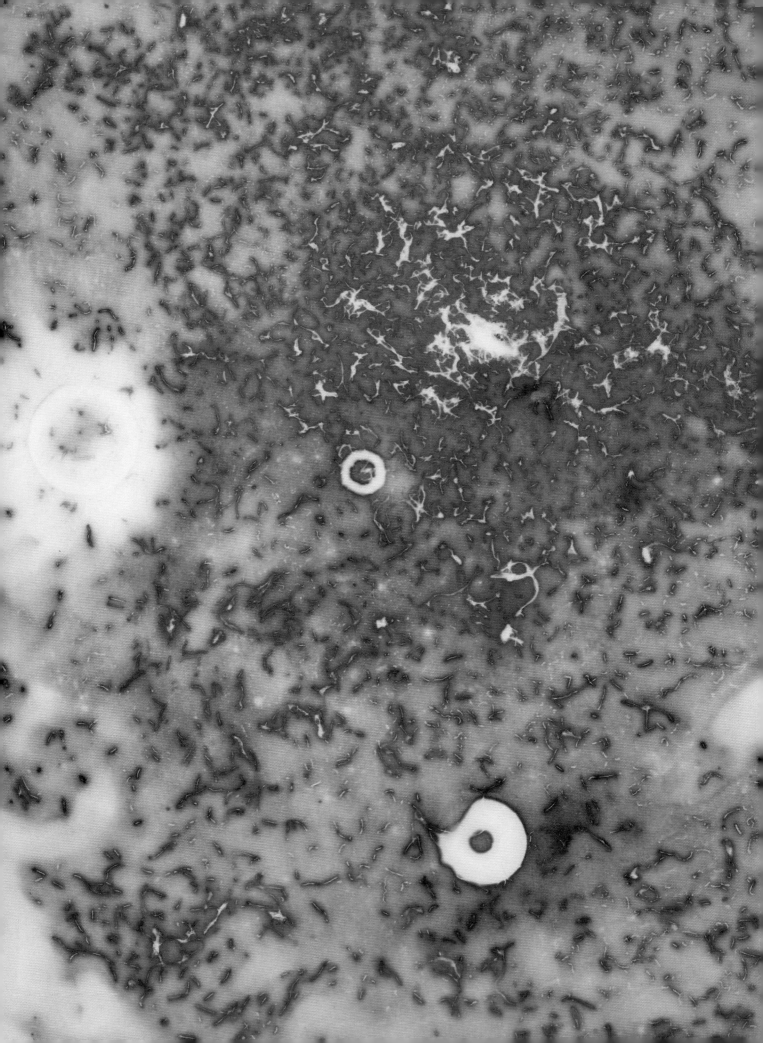

rust dyeing

You may have produced rust-dyed fabric by mistake.

Now fiber artists are making rust art by design! Using metal pans, steel wool, hardware, old grates, and rusty metal found in the street you can create lovely patterns on white or colored silk or cotton fabric. This is another technique where you can expect the unexpected to create something truly unique. Start combing the house and street for old metal!

materials and tools

Plastic cover for the table

White PFD cotton, hand-dyed fabric, or silk scarves

Tray to hold fabric (a rusty one works great)

Spray bottle

Water

White vinegar

Rubber gloves

Flat metal objects such as washers, not galvanized

Steel wool

Drawstring garbage bag large enough to fit around the tray

Heavy objects to use for pressing (optional)

Container with ¼ cup (60 ml) salt dissolved in 4 gallons (16 l) of hot water

Soap

rust dyeing

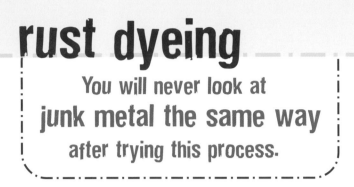

You will never look at
junk metal the same way
after trying this process.

Preparation
Protect your work surface with the plastic cover.

1

Lay the fabric on the tray. Spray it with a solution of approximately half vinegar and half water.

2

Put on rubber gloves and lay metal objects and shredded steel wool on the wet fabric. Use special care when handling metal that is already rusty. Spray again with vinegar-water.

3

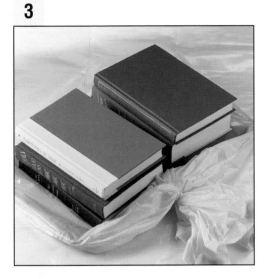

Place the tray inside the garbage bag and tie up the opening. The fabric needs to stay wet for twenty-four hours in order for the metal to rust and color the fabric. I weighted down the top of the bag with books to press the steel wool to the fabric.

4

Put on rubber gloves. Remove the bag and then remove the metal pieces and steel wool from the fabric and store them for further use. Neutralize the rust by soaking the fabric in the salt water solution. Wash the fabric in soapy water.

Susan Suggests

Be sure to use one of the fabric types listed in the materials list. They have no finishes on them that would prevent the rust from coloring the fabric.

burned-edge appliqué

Painting the silk, cutting rough shapes, and then burning the edges is a fun way to create artistic appliqués.

The singed, gray edges add a sophisticated verve to the fabric's colors. Appliqué by hand or with a sewing machine. If you stitch through the batting and backing fabric at the same time, you will complete the quilting process too! Be sure to use tweezers to hold the silk in the flame if you are doing small pieces. Have a container of water nearby in case the silk starts to burn too quickly.

Yvonne Porcella, in her book *Colors Changing Hue*, first introduced me to this method for sealing the edges of silk shapes so they could be appliquéd without turning under seam allowances.

materials and tools

Plastic cover for the table

Container with water

Scissors

Silk: natural color, 8 –12 mm

Spray bottle with water

Transparent fabric paint:
Dye-na-Flow, assorted colors

Sponge brushes: 1" (2.5 cm)

Coarse salt

Iron

Votive candle in secure, heat-proof holder

Tweezers

Backing fabric:
9½" x 12" (24.1 x 30.5 cm)

Batting:
thin, 9½" x 12" (24.1 x 30.5 cm)

Pins (optional)

Sewing machine with darning foot

Thread to match appliqués

Glue stick

Note: Pins aren't needed if you use fusible batting.

burned-edge appliqué

Salt and flame—sounds like ingredients in **a cookbook—but here is a recipe** for softly textured, vibrantly colored silk.

Preparation

Protect your work surface with the plastic cover. Have the container of water ready is case the silk starts to burn too quickly.

1

Cut several pieces of silk about 11" (27.9 cm) square and place them flat on the plastic-covered table. Spray the silk with water. Paint each piece a different color using a separate brush for each color. Spray with water again to make the paint run and puddle. Sprinkle coarse salt on the surface of the wet silk, and then let the fabric dry slowly. Remove the salt crystals and iron the silk to heat set the paint.

2

Prepare the appliqués and background pieces by cutting the painted silk into rough shapes slightly larger than you want the finished pieces to be. Don't worry about exact outlines because you will be burning the edges to get the final shape.

3

Light the candle. Using the tweezers, hold the edge of a cut silk piece horizontally in the side of the candle flame. Avoid holding the silk at the top of the flame, which will produce soot and ruin the colors. Let the silk burn just long enough to shape the piece. Rotate the piece until all the edges have been burned. The silk should stop burning as soon as you remove it from the flame, but if it continues, blow gently on it or dunk it in a container of water and try again after it dries. Keep the silk from touching the wax. Pull any crunchy bits off the edges, but avoid smearing soot onto the silk.

4

Place the backing fabric wrong side up and cover it with the batting. Position and then pin the background pieces of silk on the batting. Sew ⅛" (3 mm) from the edges of each silk piece through all the layers. Adhere the appliqué pieces to the background with the glue stick and topstitch around the edges. Cut the page to 8½" x 11" (21.6 x 27.9 cm) after stitching and finish the edges as you like.

Susan Suggests

You can use any natural-colored silk that has body. Perfect choices are China silk or silk twill of 8 to 12 mummie. (Mummie is the measure of weight for silk.)

screen printing

Screen printing is a great way to quickly apply repeated images to fabric.

You can cover a large piece of fabric for a garment or print lots of the same image on small cuts of fabric. You can make screen prints in several different ways, but some methods, such as thermography and photo emulsion, are more complex than others. Here, with simple stretcher bars and polyester mesh from the art supply store, you'll discover how to make your own screen and create images with sticky-back plastic.

materials and tools

Plastic cover for the table

Hammer

Stretcher bars: two 10" or 11"
(25.4 or 27. 9 cm) and two 12" (30.5 cm)

Scissors

Polyester mesh: 10xx – 14xx weave

Stapler

Duct tape

Toothbrush to clean mesh

Scouring powder to clean mesh

Sticky-back drawer-lining plastic

Craft knife

Newspaper

Fabric

Opaque fabric paint:
Neopaque, assorted colors

Squeegee

Bristle brush: small artist's

Iron

screen printing

With a small assembly of wood and mesh, a few **cuts in sticky-back plastic, and a handy** squeegee, create your personal style statement in cloth.

Preparation
Protect your work surface with the plastic cover.

1

Pound the stretcher bars together until the frame is tight. Cut a piece of polyester mesh to approximately the outside measurements of the frame and staple it to the wood, stretching the mesh as taut as you can. Cover all the wood frame around the mesh with duct tape, extending the tape onto the exposed mesh about ½" (1.3 cm); repeat the taping on the back of the frame. Scrub the mesh with the toothbrush and scouring powder to open all the holes in the weave completely.

2

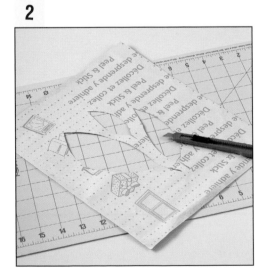

Cut a piece of sticky-back plastic slightly smaller than the outside measurements of the frame. Cut a design in the center using the craft knife. Keep the area of the design about ½" (1.3 cm) smaller than the exposed mesh on all edges. Remove the protective paper from the plastic, adhere it to the front of the mesh (the side that will be flush against the fabric), and rub it onto the mesh firmly.

3

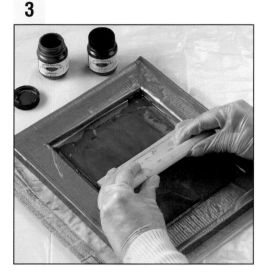

Put a thick pad of newspaper on the table and lay a piece of fabric on it, right side up. Place the frame on top of the fabric, with the design touching the fabric. Pour about 2 tablespoons (30 ml) of the paint onto the tape along one edge of the frame. The exact amount of paint you need will depend on the openness of your design. You can use two or three colors if you like. Apply firm pressure and pull the paint across the mesh with the squeegee. You may need to do two or three passes. It takes practice to know how much pressure to use, since too much will force paint underneath the edges of the design opening.

4

To avoid smearing the paint as you lift the frame, hold the fabric down with one hand and carefully pull the frame straight up. Touch up any leaks or missed spots with the brush. Continue to print images so you have a selection to choose from (you will likely have some rejects at the beginning). Let the paint dry. Scrub the screen immediately so the paint does not clog the mesh. Heat set the paint with an iron after it is completely dry.

Susan Suggests

Use a thick viscosity paint to keep the color from seeping under the edges of your design. If you do not have a squeegee, try using an old credit card.

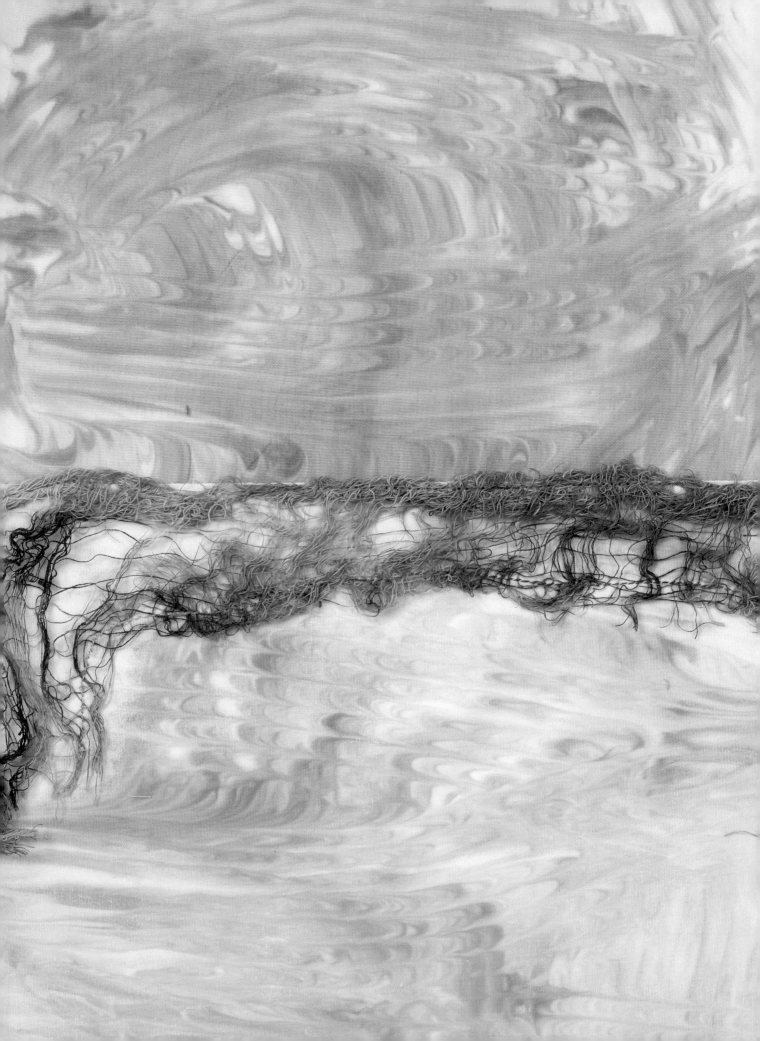

shaving cream marbling

The craft of marbling paper originated in China more than 2,000 years ago.

Marbled paper became popular in seventeenth-century Europe as a decorative finish on book covers. Paper marbling required working with a vat of a thick seaweed medium on which paint was suspended. The paint was combed to make patterns and then carefully picked up by placing a piece of paper over it. As you can imagine, there are lots of ways the process can go wrong. Here you will use foamy shaving cream for a suspension medium and drop thin paint onto the surface. Instead of paper, you will use fabric to create a unique cloth for your next project.

materials and tools

Plastic cover for the table

Foamy shaving cream

Flat plastic surface

Plastic ruler

Transparent fabric paint: Dye-na-Flow, assorted colors

Pipette or eyedropper

Coarse comb or hair pick

Fabric: white cotton or silk

Iron

shaving cream marbling

Toilette equipment has never been so glamorous!
Shaving cream and combs combine
to make the easiest marbled fabric ever.

Preparation
Protect your work surface with the plastic cover.

1 Spread enough shaving cream on the plastic surface, 1" (2.5 cm) deep, to match the size of your fabric. Smooth the top with the ruler—the top does not need to be level, just smooth.

2 Dribble straight lines of transparent paint onto the surface of the foam with a pipette or eyedropper. Use as many colors as you like.

3

Starting at one side, comb across the lines of paint, moving from the top edge to the bottom. Wipe any shaving cream off the comb. Place the comb next to the already combed area and comb from the bottom to top. Keep reversing direction as you create your design.

4

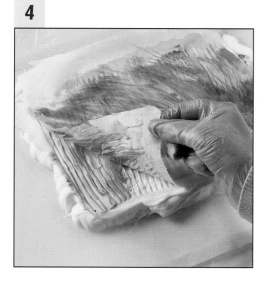

Drape a piece of fabric face down onto the surface of the foam. Press it very gently into the foam so the paint adheres to the fabric. Carefully lift the fabric off the foam and scrape the excess foam from the fabric using the ruler. Comb through the paint left on the foam and make more prints until the foam is used up, adding more paint as needed. Let the paint dry and then iron to set. Rinse and dry the fabric pieces to remove the shaving cream.

Susan Suggests

You can also comb your marbling design in a curve or a series of curves for variety.

collage with fabric

Collage has been done with paper for many years. Here we adapt it to fabric to create texture and dimension.

Most of the projects in this book involve fun and spontaneous techniques, so why not forgo the exact seam allowances, perfect corners, and precise measurements that normally make up a wall hanging and let yourself play. Collect trim, fabrics, beads, buttons, embellishments, orphan quilt blocks, fibers, and ribbon. Toss in the new techniques you've discovered in *Fabric Art Workshop*, and create a piece that tells your story!

materials and tools

Background fabric

Accent fabrics, blocks, screen prints, embroidered hankies

Trim, silk flowers and leaves, ribbon to coordinate with the fabrics

Batting: fusible, thin

Backing fabric

Iron

Glue stick or basting glue

Sewing machine

Thread

Buttons, beads, charms

collage with fabric

A project that takes us back to hunting and gathering—and helps use up the bits of ephemera we all have stashed away!

1

Select a background fabric for your collage. From your stash, gather trim, accent fabrics, buttons, anything that will coordinate with your background fabric and the theme you've chosen for the piece.

2

Cut a piece of background fabric and a piece of batting to 8½" x 11" (21.6 x 27.9 cm). Cut a backing fabric to 9½" x 12" (24.1 x 30.5 cm). Layer the background fabric (right side out), batting, and the backing fabric (right side out), and fuse them together with an iron, following the batting manufacturer's instructions.

3

Cut small pieces of accent fabrics, ribbon, and trim, and glue-baste them onto the background fabric, auditioning everything that might work. Relate elements to each other by overlapping them or connecting them with a ribbon or trim. If you have a digital camera, take photographs of different arrangements before you decide on one. Stitch around the edges or through the centers of the elements, through the batting and backing.

4

Press the extra backing fabric around to the top. Glue-baste the turned fabric to the journal page top to create a binding, folding in the corners as you go. Topstitch or satin stitch the edge of the binding. Hand sew beads, buttons, and charms onto the background fabric through all the layers.

Note: Sunprinted leaves by Diane Bartels (see Resources).

Susan Suggests

For even more freedom, try using quilt-as-you-go methods. Of course, you will want to make a larger piece after doing this journal page, and a fat quarter would be a good size for a larger background. You can either finish your project at that size or add borders or other pieces later.

A pale dawn moon—
Furrows of the new-ploughed fields
white with frost.

MEMORIES HAIKU; JOURNAL PAGES Tina Hughes

a poppy...
a field of poppies!
the hills blowing with poppies

MEMORIES HAIKU; JOURNAL PAGES Tina Hughes

MARKINGS IN THE ROCKS; COLLAGE   Susan Stein

TURQUOISE AND COPPER; WALL HANGING   Susan Stein

DREAMING OF DRAGONFLIES; QUILT   Elizabeth Lanzatella

NORTHERN LIGHTS THROUGH PINE BOUGHS; JOURNAL PAGE
Elizabeth Palmer-Spilker

MEDITATION SCREEN   Susan Stein

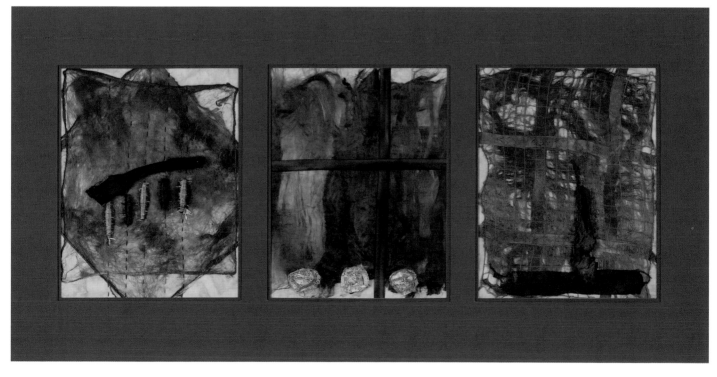

CATCH A DREAM; WALL PANEL   Susan Stein

CONTEMPORARY TECHNIQUES, TRADITIONAL CONCEPTS; QUILT
Joyce Kvaas

FLOATING LEAVES; WALL HANGING   Susan Stein

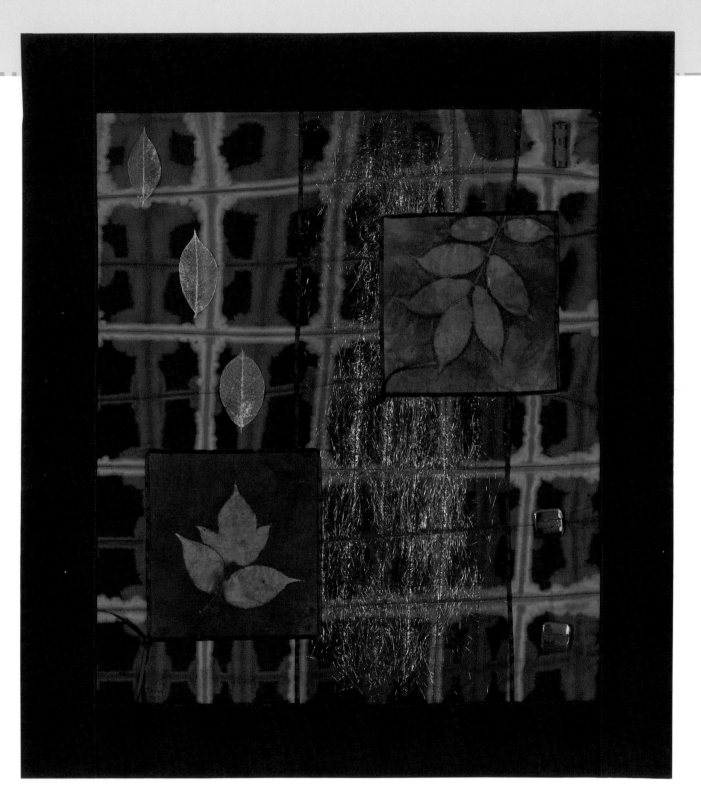

COPPER, LIGHT AND SHADOW; WALL HANGING   Susan Stein

about the author

Susan Stein started quilting in 1977 and has delighted in getting other people obsessed with quilting and surface design ever since. This former president and show chairman for Minnesota Quilters was named Minnesota Quilter of the Year in 2003. An energetic and passionate quilter, Susan has shared her talents as the author of three books and as a contributing author to numerous others. She has taught many classes in Minnesota and around the country. Many of the hundreds of quilts produced by her hands serve as wall hangings, publication pieces, and store samples, while others are on public display or in personal use. Susan co-owned a quilt shop from 1980 to 1985 and opened her current shop, Colorful Quilts and Textiles, in 1995.

resources

Sunprints, hand-dyed silk and wool fibers, hand-dyed ribbons by Diane Bartels, and most other project supplies.
Colorful Quilts & Textiles
2233 Energy Park Drive, Suite 400
St. Paul, MN 55108
651-628-9664
www.colorfulquilts.com
susan@colorfulquilts.com

Foil and foil adhesive
Laura Murray
www.lauramurraydesigns.com

Paintstiks, stencil brushes, original rubbing plates
Cedar Canyon Textiles
www.cedarcanyontextiles.com

Silk roving, cocoons, hankies, and carrier rods
Treenway Silk
www.treenwaysilks.com

ReVisions Stencils by Diane Ericson
www.dianeericson.com

**Golden Artist Colors Gel Mediums
Regular Gel (Matte)**
Available at art supply stores

Printed images
Carol Belanger Grafton, ed., *Authentic Chinese Cut-Paper Designs*, Dover Design Library (New York: Dover Publications, Inc., 1988)

index

Also Available From
Creative Publishing International

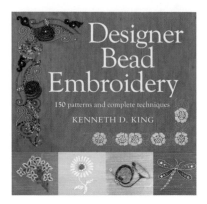

Designer Bead Embroidery
150 Patterns and Complete Techniques
by Kenneth D. King

To purchase these or other Creative Publishing International titles, contact your local bookseller, or visit our website at www.creativepub.com

Wreaths and Wallflowers
Gorgeous Decorations with Silk and Dried Florals
By Ardith Beveridge

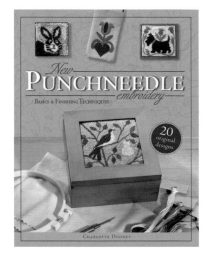

New Punchneedle Embroidery
Basics & Finishing Techniques
by Charlotte Dudney

Creative Publishing international

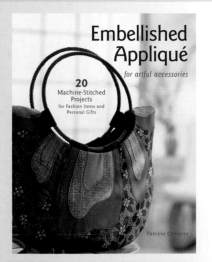

Embellished Appliqué
20 Machine-Stitched Projects for Fashion
Items and Personal Gifts
by Patricia Converse

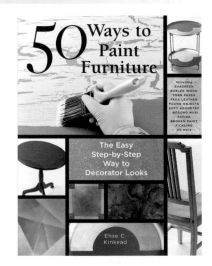

50 Ways to Paint Furniture
The Easy Step-by-Step Way to Decorator Looks
By Elise C. Kinkead